Facing The Camera
A Guide To Being Interviewed

Edward Lawrence

This book is dedicated to my Mom and Pop, Grandma D, and Grandma F. Without your support and help I would not be who I am today.

Introduction

The media is prevalent in every part of our lives whether we know it or not. We, as people, have an intense desire for knowledge. The press adds to that knowledge. Still, many of us fear the media and what the camera represents. This book will help you understand how the electronic media works and how you can benefit from *Facing the Camera*.

Table of Contents

The Camera	5
Being Interviewed	12
The Interview Look	24
The News Conference	33
The Human Element	51
The Message	61
A Final Thought	74
Lessons Learned	76

The Camera

Physically a television camera can be intimidating. It's about three feet long with a shiny glass lens at one end and a block battery attached to the other. The glare from that lens can be mentally blinding for many people, but it doesn't have to be.

The camera is a tool like any other business tool. Television journalists use that tool for their job every day, just like lawyers use word processing programs, or construction workers use hammers. The camera allows the journalist to tell the story of the day.

The story may involve your life. That frightens many people, but it shouldn't. There are easy ways to make the camera your friend. Some ways are mental others are physical.

As you look at the camera remember there is only one person behind it operating the buttons. You are only talking to that one person. Don't think about the greater implication of the camera. Don't think about all the people seeing this on their televisions or computers. In some cases a reporter will be with the photographer. Then you will be talking with him or her. You can relax and talk normally when you realize that any interview is really a one-on-one conversation.

Problems with most interviews that go wrong is you, the interviewee, are not relaxed and appear nervous. Those nerves would be understandable if you have a reason for being nervous such as you broke the law or tried to cheat someone! Then you will need an entirely new set of skills to end up looking like a rose. In all other cases take that nervous energy and use it to your advantage. For example, be conversational during the interview.

I should make a distinction here between the local media and national media. More often than not you will see members of the local media driving or walking around your town. There are fewer national media than local media representatives nation-wide. Even with all the new cable news channels, the chances of seeing a national camera crew are minimal. Still, the set up will be the same for both types of media.

Local television stations don't have the budget for a lot of people going out to cover stories. Therefore, you will see one person operating the camera, setting sound levels, and lighting. Another person will generally perform reporting duties on the local level.

On the national level the principles are the same, but networks have more money meaning more manpower. A national television crew will have one person handling the sound, probably with a boom microphone. It's a fuzzy looking microphone at the end of a long pole. The pole allows the operator to reach over something to get good sound without showing the microphone in the cameras view.

The national television crew will have a camera operator and one reporter or field producer, sometimes both. The principals are the same throughout. You are talking one-on-one with the person behind the camera or a reporter asking questions.

The goal of any crew is to ask questions to start a conversation. In most cases, for both local and national reporters the questions are to help you start talking and feel comfortable in front of the camera. The camera records the interview to get the pieces necessary to make a compelling news story. In essence the camera saves moments of everyday life that have become news worthy. That may include your opinions, information you have, or information you can get.

Chances are at some point in your life a television crew will approach you or someone you know. Many times that meeting becomes an us versus them relationship with the camera. It doesn't need to be that way. Remember if you meet a camera crew most of the people behind the camera have had the same ups and downs in their life as you have. They have the same job pressures and the same family problems. We are all human, even journalists in the media.

You can overcome any fear of going on camera. In upcoming chapters you will get basic tips for going on camera and looking good. These tips will help you prepare for an interview and will also help you physically look better on camera.

Being Interviewed

It's time. A camera crew has stopped you on the street or is coming to your office to talk. You can feel your blood pressure rise. Your nerves start jumping. Questions start running through your head. Should I have worn this shirt? What am I going to say? Will they understand what I am telling them? And that is all before the interview starts.

Relax. Take deep breaths. It will all be ok. Just remember this is going to be a conversation. Just tell the reporter what you think. If you have some expertise in an area just talk to the reporter like you would talk with your office mate or next-door neighbor. Unless of course you swear in your normal conversation, that's not something you want to do during an interview.

Just talk normally and have a conversation to get your point across. Some politicians are good at this. One of the best I have experienced was when I worked in Charlotte, NC. At the time the Mayor was Pat McCrory, who became Governor of North Carolina. He understood how to talk to the camera as if it were a friend.

For example on April 2, 2009 Mayor McCrory talked with Vice President Joe Biden. He addressed the issues of the economic stimulus with the Vice President saying Charlotte was not getting its fair share. Mayor McCrory then went on to tell reporters the money Charlotte did get wasn't being used for long-term projects. His statement was short and to the point saying, "It tends to go to short term operating needs or short term projects. We're just repaving roads as opposed to rebuilding new roads and bridges and transit."

The best stories and the best way to get your information or point of view across come from normal conversations with the reporter. Before I get into the substance of an interview there are a few basics that need to be addressed.

There are a several different types of interviews. First is the MOS as we say in the business. That stands for "man on the street" interview. These interviews are designed to be a non-scientific cross section of what the public thinks about a topic.

Everyone has an opinion. Everyone is entitled to that opinion. It amazes me how many people don't think enough of themselves to share their views. Your opinion is your opinion and it will not change whether you are talking to a reporter or your best friend.

In any event, the MOS interview is usually the fastest a journalist will do. Generally, the crew will have a certain issue, question, or topic in mind for you to talk about. This format of interview allows viewers to see and gauge what others in your area think. It exposes the audience to many different opinions.

Here's what generally happens with a MOS. This scenario is the same for local and national crews. Remember the difference with a national crew is that there may be an extra person to make sure the sound is correct on tape. You will probably be walking down the street. A reporter will walk up and ask if you have a second. The reporter will generally be holding a microphone and a cameraperson will not be far behind.

In many cases the assignment

requires that the story have a human element. I will go more in depth on this in Chapter 5 called the "Human Element". But, I remember working in Las Vegas and needing to find a certain group of tourists. I needed to talk to a British citizen because at the time that group represented the third largest international visitor to Las Vegas.

In the 100-degree heat a cameraperson and I stood on the sidewalk of a busy corner asking visitors where they were from. A couple of people confirmed they were British citizens, but did not want to share their views on why they chose Las Vegas as their tourist destination. Finally, I was able to strike up a conversation with some other British tourists and we got the interview we needed.

After you agree to give your opinion. The reporter holds up the microphone. This is where you will have to be mentally prepared. Do not be afraid of the microphone. In fact, just ignore it.

The reporter is holding the microphone up enough to hear what you have to say, but it is low enough as to not intrude on the cameraperson's shot. You do not need to bend down and talk into it. You don't need to grab it and talk into it. Just look at the reporter and have a conversation.

One misconception about the

microphone comes from entertainers. Many of us see performers holding the microphone to sing or perform. They have it so close to their mouth it looks like they are eating it. This is a specific way they need to hold it in order to sound like they do. Television does not work the same way. Think about any awards show you have seen. How funny does the presenter look when he or she gets to the podium and leans down too close to the microphone to announce the nominees?

You do not need to do that either. The stick microphone that the reporter holds is directional. The best sound comes from where it's pointing. The microphone will pick up sound on either side, but the sound is sharpest in the direction it's pointing. Therefore, a journalist can hold the microphone down a bit and still pick up sharp clear sound as you talk.

Any MOS conversation will last a maximum of five minutes. It may start with the question, "What do you think about …?" Generally the reporter just needs to hear what you have to say about the topic and then moves on to the next person. In any story the more people the reporter talks to, the more opinions that can be gathered. Viewers will benefit from hearing a wide range of opinions.

There is also the confrontation interview. In that case a reporter and cameraperson will walk up to you with cameras already rolling. The worst thing you can do is hold your hand up to block the lens. That makes you look guilty of something, even if you are not. If you choose to answer the questions from the reporter remember to look at the reporter. Do not look around. That will make you look shifty! Answer the questions the reporter has using the technique described in the chapter titled "The Message." After answering a few questions it is ok to walk off. Just remember not to be combative. The reporter might try to be combative with the questions. The old adage 'you attract more bees with honey' holds true. Be nice and the reporter might be the one who comes off looking like a bully. The viewers will decide.

Another type of interview to get a message out is a news conference. It allows you to talk once and relay the information to all the interested television stations at the same time. The news conference will be handled at greater length in a later chapter of the book.

Sometimes a crew will show up at your home or office for a "sit down" interview. This type of interview will be used within an edited story. In this case you need to pick the right spot. Depth of field makes the one-on-one interview stand out. If you have your back against a white wall then it will look as if you are in jail. The camera only sees the portion of the wall behind your head. The farther the background is from you the more the camera will see. The longer distance also gives it a softer focus. That means you will be in focus as the interviewee, but the background might be a little fuzzy. This depth of field gives you the best "look" in an interview.

The Interview Look

In order to look good during that one-on-one interview for a reporter's edited story, there are a few things you can do. The first thing to do is relax. Take several deep breaths before the interview begins. Believe you are having a friendly conversation with the person next to or behind the camera. Forget the camera is there. Mentally block everything out. Don't listen to the clicking of the camera. Don't look at the microphone. Forget about the lights. Just concentrate on the question being asked. That should help you ignore the rest of what is around you.

Look directly at the reporter to have

your conversation. It may feel a bit awkward with all of the commotion going on around you, but you must think about how it will look in the 37-inch TV box. Almost all interviews, except those done by in studio anchors where the interview subject is talking to the anchor directly over satellite, will be conducted with the interviewee looking at the interviewer.

The reason to look at the reporter goes to the psychology of the audience. Since it's an edited story, only the reporter addresses the audience. The audience watches the reporter's edited version of the facts, evidence, and interviews related to the story. Then the reporter delivers the information for the viewers to decide. The viewers watch the reporter present the information he or she gathered related to the story and form their own opinions. If you, the interviewee, want to drive home your opinion you need to look directly at the reporter to make a strong showing in your part of the story.

In order to look your best on camera there are a few tricks of the trade. Watch your local news anchor for some hints. Look closely and you will notice a few things. Anchors will be sitting forward. That slight move does a couple of useful things for your look on television.

Television is two-dimensional. You must give it the third dimension by slightly sitting forward. Sitting forward gives the illusion of weight reduction. As a male anchor or reporter leans slightly into the camera the shadows under his chin will also disappear, hiding some weight in the upper neck and under the chin. This trick works for pictures but more importantly works during an interview.

In watching the news you will notice some people being interviewed breaking this rule by leaning back. When you lean back, shadows form under the chin making it appear as if there is more skin. It gives the impression of a double chin.

I have interviewed many people who have been guilty of this backward lean. Many of those offenders are attorneys I have interviewed over the years. A number of them love to show off a massive office, nice desk, and the vanity wall of honors and diplomas. In that environment the attorney feels at home. The comfort level provides a relaxed atmosphere, but allows for bad habits to slip into the interview.

One of those habits is leaning back in their chair as we discussed. The other bad habit is swiveling. It feels comfortable, but can be very distracting on television. The viewer will look at the interview and become dizzy. Small movements are exaggerated on television. The swivel makes it look like there might be an earthquake happening as the interview takes place!

As you watch the news, a trick you will not notice right away is a male anchor sitting on his jacket tail. This action will smooth out the jacket on camera. Clothes tend to bunch if you sit for a longer period and move naturally. By sitting on the tail of your jacket the shoulders appear non-wrinkled and non-bunched. It pulls on the back of the jacket leaving nice lines under your arms.

For women, some of these tips get a little trickier. Leaning forward slightly is a good idea. It has the same slimming effect on a woman's face as on a man's. When it comes to women's clothes, there is more of a grey area on what to wear. As men do, some women have suit jackets in their closets. The trick of sitting on the tail of the jacket works only if that tail is long enough. Women also wear dresses, blouses, and sweaters.

As a woman, if you know you are going to be interviewed it's safest to dress conservatively. A top cut too low will not look good as too much skin might distract viewer's eyes. A shiny necklace will sparkle in the camera and should be taken off. It can also distract from your comments.

Ostentatious earrings will be a distraction. If your longer earrings dangle in the interview as you move your head to talk, the viewer will be fixated on the movement not what you are saying.

In one Arizona interview, a member of the U.S. House of Representatives wanted to talk about a project she was proud of in the northern Arizona area. She put on her best business suit with very nice long silver earrings. They had large silver circles on the ends, which almost touched her shoulders. As she spoke, the earrings moved back and forth. The interview was outside near one of the projects she wanted to promote.

The sun was in the perfect spot and reflected slightly in the large silver circles. As she tried to extol the virtues of her accomplishment, beams of sun gleamed from just above her shoulders. Her message was lost to the viewer.

The last physical tip for men and women has to do with eye contact. When being interviewed always look at the reporter. If you move your eyes around looking at the reporter, cameraperson, wall, or anything else in the room you will look shifty. Remember, the camera amplifies every movement. Your message will be lost in the distraction.

The News Conference

When you have a situation that requires giving the same information to many different news outlets at the same time, a news conference is one way to handle it. At a news conference, you will not have to repeat yourself. Here you gather all the media together in one room to address them and take questions. I do not advocate this method because it is very impersonal.

Another option, though technically not a news conference, is by talking one-on-one with a reporter. The viewers get the sense that you, as the interviewee, are answering all of the reporter's questions.

It does not seem that you are making a detached statement, as is the case with a formal news conference.

In this scenario, holding one-on-one interviews with many reporters can be time consuming if there are a lot of people wanting your attention, but it will look better.

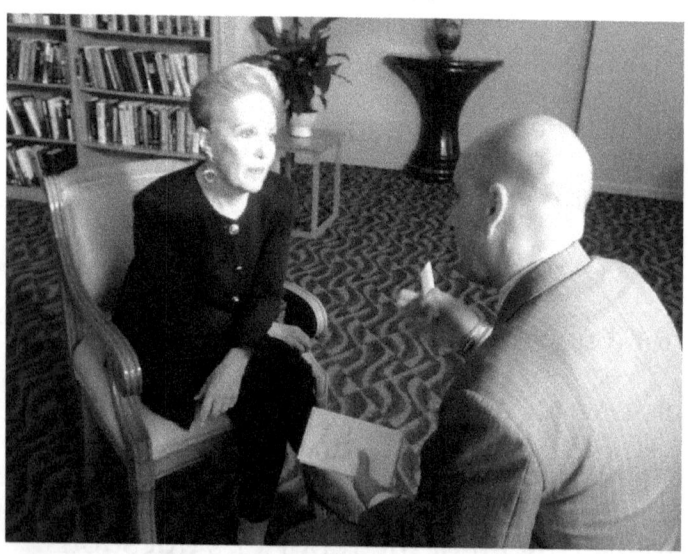

One-on-one interview with Dear Abby on June 13, 2010.

Movie executives understand this technique. This is one of the reasons the studios do "junkets". A junket helps promote a movie. The studio has one or more celebrities in a room where they can give interviews and reporters have a specific time slot to interview each of them.

The studio will set up two cameras. There will be lights and two chairs. One chair is for the reporter and one chair is for the celebrity. I have done many 'junkets' over the years. They can be time consuming and repetitive for the celebrity, but in the end the one-on-one interaction gives a more personal feel for viewers of each entertainment news outlet.

The entertainment reporters are given between three and five minutes with the celebrity. Like a factory, the movie studio floor manager moves the interviews along. Before the reporter leaves, the studio gives him/her two flash drives with their interview on it. Each drive has one camera angle. An editor can then match up the sound so you can have the reporter asking the question on camera and cut to the celebrity answering it.

If using this technique, make sure to give the crew a chance to set up extra lights. In this setting the lights can soften facial features and enhance a background so the interviewee pops out on the screen.

No one understands the technique of one-on-one news interviews better than the executives at MGM-Mirage in Las Vegas. After making the announcement that they will spend more than $7 billion dollars to buy Mandalay Resort Group, the top financial officer made time for every local television station and interested national channels to ask questions.

His message was not lost and the executive was able to connect with the audience as if one-on-one. It also set up a rapport with the local reporters who cover the mega casino company. That opens an avenue for the large Las Vegas employer to talk to workers as well as others who rely on the company in the community.

Sometimes mass news conferences are unavoidable. This is especially true if there is a major incident. If you must go down this road, there are a few critical things to remember. We have all seen the cluster of microphones on a stand. All of those microphone flags clutter the screen and in some cases you cannot see the person talking. This is sloppy, though sometimes a must in a breaking news situation. Make sure the microphone stand is low enough so that the face of the shortest person is viewable. In a situation like this, it's also best not to let it get out of control. Reporters are aggressive people by nature. If there is no plan for the news conference they will talk over each other trying to get their question answered. Make sure in the beginning you set the rules.

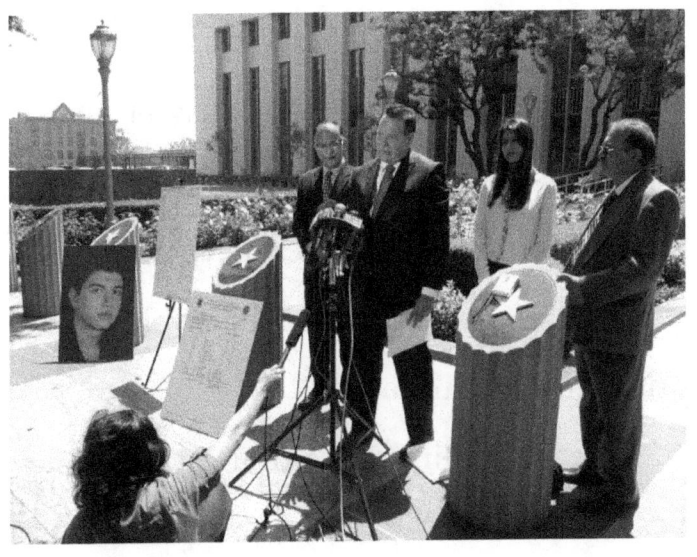

News Conference on June 18, 2012 at LA Federal Court.

For instance, in April of 2013 when the fertilizer plant in West, TX exploded killing 15 people and leveling half the town of West, the media descended on the area. The Sheriff made it clear from the outset that he would answer questions, but only questions from reporters who raised their hands and were called on. To his credit the Sheriff sometimes stood at the microphone for an hour answering everyone's questions. He minimized the chaos and defused a potentially ugly situation by calling on those people who only raised their hand.

It was a different situation the same year when Lindsay Lohan went to one of her many probation violation hearings. Her New York attorney flew to Los Angeles. Since he was short and the microphone flags covered the bottom part of his face. Then he allowed the news conference to became a free-for-all of reporters shouting questions at him. The tension in the air escalated as reporters shouted louder and louder. In some cases, reporters started asking questions before he finished his last answer. In the news business, this is called "stepping on the bite." It became hard to get a good sound bite from the attorney. When he finally got frustrated and walked off, not only did it look as if he stonewalled reporters by walking off abruptly, but reporters ran after him still shouting questions.

In an ideal situation you will have time to plan a major news conference. There are a few key factors you will need so everything starts out smoothly. The first vital factor is about the location.

The same depth of field rules for the one-on-one interview apply to a news conference. Try to find a location that has enough room to spread out. As with the one-on-one interview, the farther away the background, the less it will look as if the person being interviewed is standing in a jail cell. If the wall is right behind the podium it will accentuate the two-dimensional feel on the television screen.

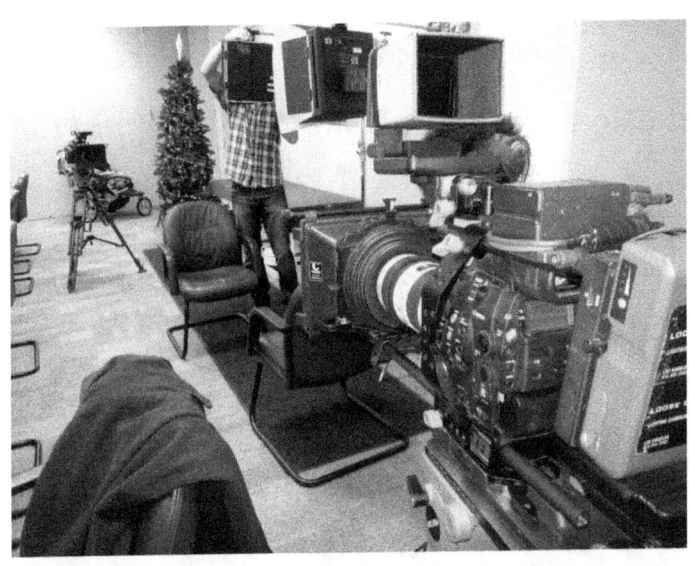

One-on-one interview at Union Rescue Mission Dec 6, 2013.

Even red carpet walks at award ceremonies use depth of field. When I covered the Academy of Country Music Awards in 2013 for CBS, the red carpet itself was about 20 feet wide. Our cameras were on one side. The wall with the ACM logo was on the other. Those 20 feet made a huge difference and allowed the country music stars to stand out visually. It put the background softly out of focus so the viewer's eye naturally trained on the person being interviewed.

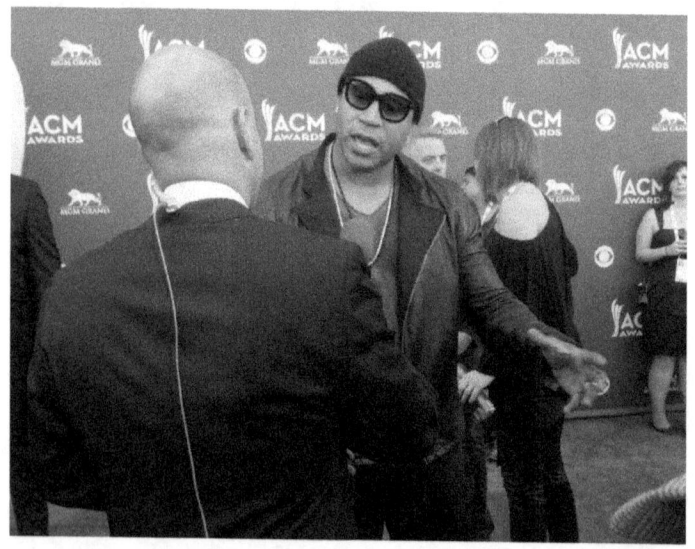

Interview with LL Cool J at ACM Awards April 7, 2013.

In a news conference you want to minimize the number of microphone flags that clutter the person being interviewed. The microphone flags of some stations are so large and visually loud that the viewers end up losing the message because they try to read the microphone flags. Radio stations are notorious for having the largest most obnoxious microphone flags. Those stations do that on purpose to try and get the free advertising offered when there is a cluster of flags on a microphone stand or podium.

A malt box to connect to the microphone cables will solve the problem. You can rent one fairly cheaply. It usually comes in a suitcase. Opening the suitcase will reveal dozens of XLR cable inputs that TV crews and radio reporters can plug into for sound. It works off one microphone on the podium. Some larger police departments have perfected this technique. Although those same departments, while getting points for uncluttering the podium, get poor marks for depth of field.

When the Los Angeles Police Department or LAPD holds a news conference, there are so many stations in the LA area interested in covering it that 20 television cameras could show up. The police have a portable malt box for all the necessary microphone cables. The new Downtown LAPD police headquarters also has a room wired for sound. The XLR microphone plugins line the wall. In either case the face of the police chief, or whoever provides the interview, remains unobstructed. That allows the viewer to focus on the message when the story airs, not the bright colors of the different news outlets' microphone logos.

When setting up for any news conference, you must remember the lighting. In many cases photographers from the various news outlets will have lights they can set up to face the interview subject. In television you want to make sure the lights facing the interviewee are brighter than the light behind the person. If the news conference is "backlit," then you will not see anything but a silhouette. In that scenario, there is so much light behind him or her that the iris on the camera closes to adjust to the brightness. That, in turn, makes whoever is in the frame darker. In many cases, it means you can't see the person's face at all. Make sure the background is darker than the light coming in from the front.

In 2000, Al Gore ran for President as the Democratic Party's nominee. I covered a rally he held to gain support in Charlotte, NC. The rally took place in a thrift shop that helped homeless people get jobs. The press secretary decided to hold the event on the loading dock area of the thrift shop. It was a large warehouse that had a covered loading dock. One side opened to the outside so 18-wheelers could back in and unload merchandise. There were almost no lights in the dock area. To this day I have no idea why, but the press secretary decided to have then Presidential hopeful Gore's back to the street.

The reporter's backs were to the store while standing on the loading dock area. As a result, the Carolina sun backlit the candidate and our photographers were pleading with the press secretary to flip the scene. That would have provided natural light on Gore's face. But the secretary insisted it stay as is. You guessed it! The photographers had two options. Option one was manually closing the iris on the camera making Gore look so dark that he looked like just a shadow standing on the dock. Option two was opening the iris until you could see the candidate's face. That made the background so washed out it looked like Gore was speaking from the sun. It distracted the viewer's focus from the then Vice President and his message. All they could see was bright white behind him. It was so white you could not even see the trees across the street.

The bottom line is be smart and your message will be properly delivered with the best quality video and without distractions.

The Human Element

When we talk about the human element, whether it's the reporter doing the interview or disruptive members of the public, many factors come into play. In those cases it would make sense to know with whom you are speaking. The reporter who conducts the interview makes all the difference in the experience for the interviewee. In most cases the reporter tends to be a stand up person looking to accurately tell both sides of the story.

There are a few cases of reporters trying to make a name for themselves and doing it at the expense of an interviewee. I will not name anyone, but I used to work with a reporter who thought the only way to do an interview was to constantly aggravate the person being interviewed. In every story, from road closures to features on community events, he tried to ask the most absurd leading questions just to make the person being interviewed angry. There are certainly times when a reporter needs to be tough on an interview subject, such as when a person breaks the law or an elected leader needs to be held accountable for a vote or an action. Then it is fair to "go after" an interviewee. In most cases an interview is just a discussion that is part of a puzzle that pulls the story together.

If you have advance warning for an interview, I suggest firing up your computer, going on a station's website to watch a few stories by the reporter coming to your office or home. You will get a feel for what type of person the reporter will be when he or she shows up.

I try to make my interview subject feel as comfortable as possible. I will talk with them before about life or something funny that just happened. I realized long ago, if you spend ten extra minutes with someone, you can get a really good story. In many cases that will put the person you are interviewing at ease. I tell them to try to ignore the camera and lights. It's just a one-on-one conversation with a friend.

When you relax while being interviewed you sound better, look more comfortable, and will be able to suppress the nerves. It can be a nerve-racking thing facing the camera.

Instead of the one-on-one interview, you might take part in a news conference where it's impossible to tell which reporters will be showing up and asking questions. If you have to do a news conference one way to minimize the human element is to hold it inside. In a larger city you start to have issues with non-news people coming around. Some of them think it's funny to disrupt a news conference. In other cases you will have non-news people trying to make a name for themselves, shouting absurd questions, or trying to disrupt the speaker from getting their message out.

There have been countless times over the years where an outdoor news conference has become a circus sideshow. I have discovered that public disruptions happen fewer times in smaller cities. In my experience, in a large city, there is more potential for something to go wrong on a public street. It happens a lot when the news conference takes place outside a courthouse and there is no organized or controlled framework established.

In 2013, I covered the civil lawsuit brought by Katherine Jackson against AEG Live. The suit blamed AEG Live for the death of Katherine's son Michael Jackson. Jackson died in June of 2009 from an overdose of Propofol. A jury found that Dr. Conrad Murray administered the dangerous drug to help the King of Pop sleep, but could not wake Jackson up in the morning.

Katherine Jackson tried to show in her lawsuit that Dr. Murray was actually an employee of AEG Live. The lawsuit claimed that as an employee AEG Live would be responsible for Dr. Murray's actions. She also tried to show that AEG Live pressured her son too much and that both of those factors led to his death. The jury ended up siding with AEG Live and no damages were awarded.

During the civil trial Katherine Jackson's attorneys held a few news conferences outside the courthouse. At one of them people with signs showed up trying to get in the background. A non-news person started shouting while the attorney was in the middle of his statement. It cut the news conference short and the message from the attorney was muddled.

Another classic problem happened when I covered one of the Lindsay Lohan's appearances in court. She had to go before an LA County Judge in 2013 for parole violations. The violations stemmed from a series of incidents after police arrested her for driving under the influence and crashing her Porsche into a wall at the Beverly Hills Hotel. At one of the final times she had to appear her attorney, brought in from New York City, held a news conference to explain a deal he struck with the court to keep Lindsay out of jail and get her into rehab.

It was held outside the courthouse near the airport in Los Angeles. As the attorney started talking, Michael Lohan barged loudly through the row of cameras set up on tripods facing the attorney. He could have come from the side where there were no cameras set up. Michael Lohan started shouting at the attorney saying the lawyer did not make this deal with Lindsay Lohan's approval. Her father was yelling that she was blindsided in court by her attorney and did not know what was going on. Michael Lohan got so close to the attorney it looked like he actually might do physical harm to the attorney. Someone with Lohan pulled him back and the attorney abruptly walked away from the microphones mid-sentence. It made for great reality TV, but did nothing to help the message the attorney was trying to convey.

In public, the human factor can be severely disruptive to an interview. When possible, it's best to have the news conference or interview in a controlled environment where antics can't take away from the news.

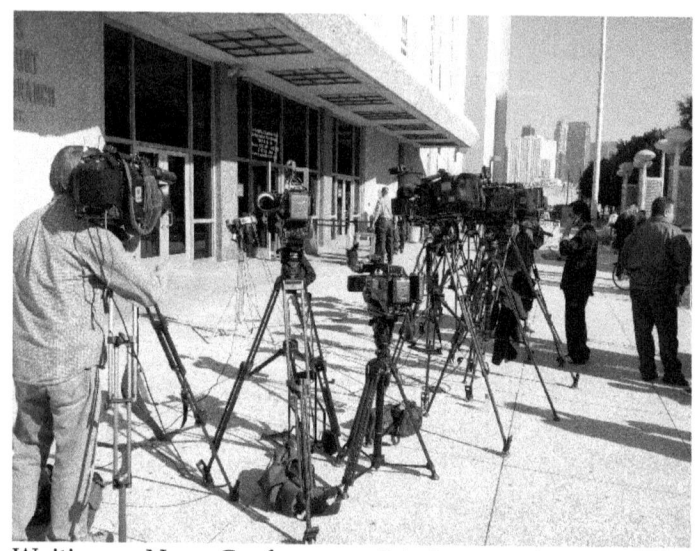
Waiting on News Conference at LA Courts Feb 12, 2012

The Message

The message will be the single most important tool you will need in a televised interview. There will be times you have only seconds to prepare for an interview. There will also be times where you have hours, even days, to prepare. In all cases make sure your message is clear and concise.

When MTV started, many people blamed the channel for shortening everyone's attention span. Whether it was a result of the cable music video channel or just the natural evolution caused by our fast-paced lives, attention spans have decreased over the years.

Many news outlets have targeted their product around the shorter attention span of news consumers. For example, you will rarely find USA Today articles continuing onto second and third pages. During local news ten years ago a VO (voice over) read by the anchor would have been one minute long. In general, it is now between 20 and 30 seconds. Reporters in most newsrooms are now slated 1:20 to 1:30 for their stories on tape. That number is down from two minutes in the early 2000's.

All of this means your message will have to be targeted and well thought out. If you take a stopwatch to any national newscast you will see an interesting pattern. When a reporter has a taped story, time how long the actual interview subject stays on the screen. It's the same when the anchor reads a VOSOT (Voice Over Sound On Tape), where he/she reads a story, then stops talking, and an interviewee starts talking. When the interview is over the anchor will finish the story. You will find interview subjects are on within the story for eight seconds or less.

During the interview a reporter is listening to what you are saying, but also listening for that quick, concise, sound bite of eight seconds or less. When you prepare for an interview think about the central message you would like to get across to the viewers. That message must then be whittled down into basically one or possibly two quick sentences. When in a one-on-one interview go back to that central theme. Whatever the question might be, work the answer back around to that central theme in the eight second sound bite you identified to get your message across.

This eight second rule applies whether you have a one-on-one interview or a news conference. It doesn't matter if you are sitting down for the interview or standing up. You need an eight second moment during the interview to catch the reporter's ear and the viewer's attention.

Politicians get interviewed all the

time. You would guess they are some of the best at targeting the eight second message. Some are good at it. A vast majority of the politicians I interviewed could not get their message across.

One of my most difficult interviews when it came to picking sound bites was former Governor of Nevada Kenny Guinn. His background was in teaching. He became superintendent of the Clark County School System and then eventually Governor of Nevada from 1999 to 2007.

I interviewed him a dozen or more times. Every time he started on a topic his comments soon wandered. He would start a good sound bite, get about four seconds into it, then stop and start talking about how it reminded him of a story from when he was a teacher. His stories would ramble on for ten minutes sometimes. He would eventually go back to the topic, but not in complete thoughts. It was extremely difficult to get any concise message from this interview.

The former Mayor of Las Vegas Oscar Goodman was one of the best at giving sound bites during an interview. For example, I interviewed the Mayor in February of 2009 after President Barack Obama criticized Las Vegas by saying, "When times are tough, you tighten your belts. You don't go buying a boat when you can barely pay your mortgage. You don't blow a bunch of cash on Vegas when you're trying to save for college."

Immediately Mayor Goodman defended his city in an interview I did. He asked the President for an apology and said in an interview with me, "It breaks my heart that people are being fired and laid off from their jobs. This will contribute to that. So, my job is to straighten it out."

That sound bite is less than eight seconds. It shows emotion and viewers everywhere could relate to it. It was a mastery of a media interview that got his message across in a memorable way. The reverberations went to the US Senate floor, the White House, and the

President's upcoming State of the Union message that omitted any reference to Las Vegas.

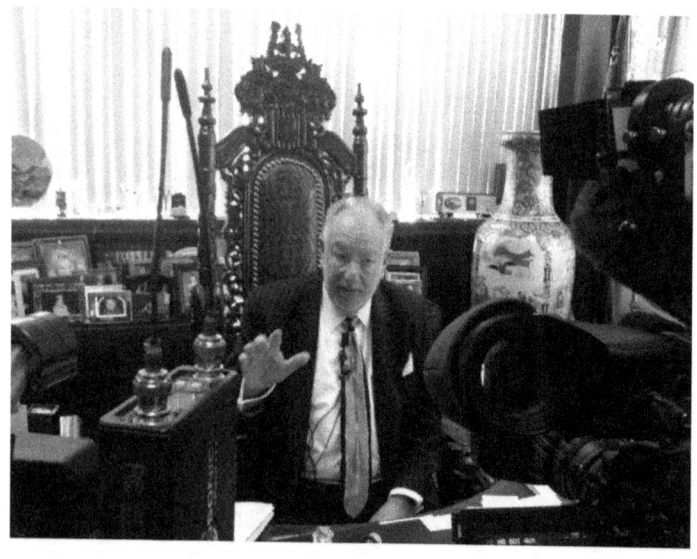

Las Vegas Mayor Oscar Goodman in his office Dec 10, 2009.

Although Mayor Goodman offered good sound bites, sometimes he did not think before he spoke and his comments got him in trouble. One of the most memorable comments came in November of 2005. The Mayor was fed up with taggers. Those are the criminals who deface property with a spray can. The City of Las Vegas spent hundreds of thousands of dollars beautifying highway landscaping projects. Taggers went to work, in some cases, the day after a project was finished and defaced it. When interviewed about the problem Mayor Goodman said, "These punks come along and deface it. I am saying maybe you put them on TV and cut off a thumb that may be the right thing to do." That is a great sound bite about eight seconds long. The comment got Goodman in trouble, started a national debate about cruel punishment, and the damages taggers cause.

The comment also shows another characteristic of a good sound bite. It shows emotion. A reporter is looking for the emotion in the interview to come across. In the story, the reporter can give all the facts and numbers that might be in the interview, but that stuff is boring to viewers. What captures attention is a short message that can relay a feeling. In Mayor Goodman's comment, you can hear the exasperation of trying to fix the damage caused by taggers. It's short and to the point. Everyone remembered what he said.

The best interviewees can always come back to that eight second sound bite.

No matter what question is asked you can start answering it, but remember to return to your central theme. Be careful not to be too staged or robotic about it. Your message should not be the same "catch phrase" over and over. Then the interview will feel too canned.

Decide what your message is and use it as a central theme, not the same exact words. Remember from the beginning of this book, you want to talk with the reporter or reporters as if they are friends. Be relaxed. Don't be afraid to show a little emotion to get your message across. As you formulate the message, remember to speak as if you were talking with friends.

The news is written for a seventh grade level. That means your message and conversation has be something a seventh grader can understand, no matter what the topic. Formulating a message and getting it across are not easy things. Sometimes if you remember the message as a theme and just relax, the eight second sound bite will develop organically through the course of the conversation.

There is one exception to the eight second rule. You could be involved in an extended conversation where you are live in a studio or on a remote satellite. In those cases you could be talking directly into the camera with the anchor in another city. This whole interview will break the eight second rule, but you still need to remember it. When you do interviews like that, chances are, an editor will cut the video down and use it for a later show. If you weave your eight second sound bite in, that snippet might be replayed over and over all day or for several days depending on the story.

So, in this case, you still need to remember to have a central message you can get across in eight seconds. Chances are that will be the clip that runs in later shows from the extended interview.

A Final Thought

Doing an interview for television could prove to be one of the most important things you do in your lifetime. Embrace it and use the opportunity to share your message. It could lead to a small victory or great things down the road.

Someone might see the interview and say they need to hire that person. It might increase your standing as an expert in whatever field you work. It could be the publicity you need to make the next step in your career or life.

Doing an interview is not as scary as it seems if you are mentally prepared, ready with your look, have figured out your central theme, and can get it out in eight seconds!

Lessons Learned

The Camera:

1. Tool used by journalists that has a lens and a battery
2. Remember the interview is a one-on-one conversation.
3. Be conversational during the interview.
4. Don't fear the camera.

Being Interviewed:

1. Treat as a conversation.
2. Avoid leaning into the microphone.
3. Know interview types:
    a. Man on the Street
    b. Confrontation

    c. News Conference

    d. Sit-down.

The Interview Look:

1. Relax.
2. Concentrate on the question.
3. Address the interviewer.
4. Avoid swiveling or fidgeting if seated.
5. Be smart about clothing.
6. Make Eye contact and don't look around.

The News Conference:

1. Conducting one-on-one interviews is more personal.

2. Establish News Conference Location; It Matters. News conference Location matters.
3. Deliver a clear message with a structured News Conference.

The Human Element:

1. Know with whom you are speaking.
2. Be comfortable as interviewee for best message.
3. Consider the human element when selecting a location.

The Message:

1. Get your message out in eight seconds.
2. Show emotion.

3. Return to the eight second message.
4. Avoid canned answers.

About The Author

Edward is an EMMY award winning journalist who has been breaking news to U.S. audiences for over two decades. As a freelance Correspondent for CBS News, his stories have been seen within the local news of CBS stations across the nation. His work also has been on the CBS Evening News and CBS This Morning.

He has covered a wide range of news. New Year's Eve of 2013 CBS appointed Edward to handle the live shots for their stations around the nation, from Times Square. Always on the front lines of the biggest stories, his coverage has included the West, TX fertilizer plant explosion, the arrests of the Boston bombing suspects and Oklahoma's EF5 tornadoes.

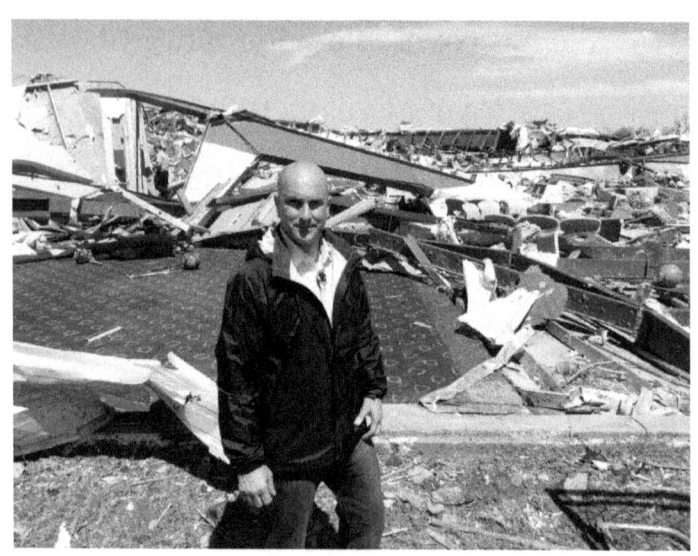

Photo from Moore, OK after EF5 Tornado May 22, 2013.

Before climbing to the network level, Edward worked as a freelance Reporter for KCBS / KCAL, reporting the news for viewers in the Los Angeles area.

His early news career has spanned stints at CBS stations in Charlotte, NC and Las Vegas, NV as a Reporter/Fill-in Anchor. While there, he covered some of the most memorable stories in the history of those cities—including the murder trial of former NFL Player Rae Carruth and the racing death of Charlotte Hornet Bobby Phills. In Las Vegas, he reported the 100 year flooding in the city, as well as the conviction of former football star OJ Simpson.

Credibility built on years of experience and a dedication to uncovering and delivering the facts for viewers, drive Edward's career. He works to present all sides so viewers can make up their own minds and strives to tell stories that impact the world.

www.ingramcontent.com/pod-product-compliance
Lightning Source LLC
Chambersburg PA
CBHW051815170526
45167CB00005B/2019